THE CUCKOO'S HAIKU

and Other Birding Poems

each bird's name you say
recalls the one who first called
your name to hear it

For Joel Wachtel and Jim Caldwell, teachers and friends
M. J. R.

For Daisy
S. F.

Text copyright © 2009 by Michael J. Rosen
Illustrations copyright © 2009 by Stan Fellows

First edition 2009

Library of Congress Cataloging-in-Publication Data is available.

Library of Congress Catalog Card Number 2008021417

ISBN 978-0-7636-3049-2

2 4 6 8 10 9 7 5 3 1

Printed in China

This book was typeset in Golden Cockerel and Sudestada.
The illustrations were done in watercolor and pencil.

Candlewick Press
99 Dover Street
Somerville, Massachusetts 02144

visit us at www.candlewick.com

THE CUCKOO'S HAIKU
and Other Birding Poems

Michael J. Rosen *illustrated by* Stan Fellows

CANDLEWICK PRESS

Spring

Eastern Bluebird

Canada Goose

American Goldfinch

Northern Cardinal

American Crow

Ruby-throated Hummingbird

Mourning Dove

on a staff of wires
blue notes inked from April skies
truly, spring's first song

Eastern Bluebird

chestnut throat,
breast, and flanks

males are darker,
bright blue

bluebirds are thrushes,
related to robins

Canada Goose

eleven different subspecies are known:
the farther north, the smaller the bird.

the pond's still airstrip
far-off trumpets grow louder —
one *splash!* two . . . hushed . . . glides . . .

white chinstrap, black head —
male and female identical

above gold jonquils
feeding finches stacked like coins
April's alchemy

American Goldfinch

travel in
small groups:
feeder is a tower of gold

funny—their song is
"potato-chips, potato-chips"

first feeders at dawn
paired like red quotation marks
last feeders at dusk

male redder, female more blushing gray
with red tail and wings; cone-shaped bill,
also red

Northern Cardinal

song:
"what cheer, cheer,
cheer, cheer"

blooming apple tree
round and white as one peeled fruit
crow-seeds at its core

American Crow

huge violet-black birds

(commonly eighteen inches tall, with a wingspan twice that)

the apple tree is all blossom, just hints of green

outside your window
the first mowers of spring? no . . .
hummingbirds are back!

Ruby-throated
Hummingbird

song: fast, squeaky chipping
also the hum/buzz of
their wings' vibration

male has brilliant metallic-ruby throat
(called gorget), the larger female
has white throat

windowsill dove nest
all month, no breeze comes inside
we wait to be hatched

Mourning Dove

males have bluish crown, pinkish breast
(small head for such a large bird)

females can have five or six clutches
in one year; each lasts a month.
(two weeks brooding, two weeks feeding)

Summer

Chimney Swift

Belted Kingfisher

Barred Owl

Great Blue Heron

Pileated Woodpecker

Northern Mockingbird

Common Grackle

myriad specks of mosquitoes, too small to draw

twittering at dusk
chimney swifts sail above the
citronella glow

Chimney Swift

nickname: flying cigar

sound is a high-pitched, rapid twitter

the trapeze itself
kingfisher swings tree to tree
fish catch in his fall

frowsy-headed bird
of gray-blue and white

chestnut-colored
bellyband

Belted
Kingfisher

who cooks for you, who . . .
far, then close, the barred owls call
"come listen," I call

females larger,
weighing more than two pounds;
wingspan can be over three and a half feet

round, heart-shaped face;
no ear tufts

Barred Owl

heron zigzag-stalks
no ripples around its legs
try to hold that   still

largest heron; widespread throughout North America

white stripe on crown,
black plume feathers behind eye
extend off the neck

gray bird with bluish gray on
abdomen and wings (can have
six-and-a-half-foot wingspan)

Great Blue
Heron

woodpecker *knock-knocks* . . .
riddled with the same question
trees yawn, answering

nearly a foot and a half tall

makes holes up to one foot long up and down a tree

Pileated
Woodpecker

Drumming loud, two to three
seconds long, then fading

often imitates backyard noises — even a sprinkler!

Northern Mockingbird

these birds can move!

acrobatic flyers!

great hoppers!

wings closed, they even "parachute" to the ground!

the one-man bird band:
diva, choir, and orchestra
unbroken record

splashing in the road
asphalt-black grackle — takes off
leaving the pothole

Common Grackle

large, iridescent blackbird — purple and bronze! —
with long black beak

harsh song is a rusty gate:
"readle-eak!"

Autumn

Cedar Waxwing

White-breasted Nuthatch

European Starling

American Robin

Black-billed Cuckoo

the great oak's tresses
beaded with cedar waxwings
wind tossing its head

tips of wing feathers look dipped in reddish sealing wax; tail tip is yellow
(or orange if the bird has been eating honeysuckle berries)

Cedar Waxwing

black mask
with white outline

sounds are very
high: "bzeee!"

gravity's jester
the nuthatch orbits a branch
worlds away, but here

White-breasted Nuthatch

song is a muffled "what, what, what"

often, its very short, tail points up,
and its cap (black for males,
gray for females) points down

bill yellow in breeding season; white-spotted feathers take on green and purple sheen

masking the daylight
one wheeling black star explodes
thousands of starlings

European Starling

*juvenile's breast is spotted;
turns solid rust-red in spring*

two dappled stragglers:
bright poison ivy berries
young robin eating

song is:
"cheerily, cheer up, cheer up,
cheerily, cheer up!"

American Robin

the cuckoo's haiku
hidden like the chance of rain
its name, repeating

Black-
billed
Cuckoo

only seventeen days from egg to flying from the nest—among the shortest of any bird

this species has
a close relative:
the Yellow-billed
Cuckoo (top bill black,
bottom mandible yellow);
has pinkish orange
wing patches

Winter

Dark-eyed Junco

Wild Turkey

Blue Jay

House Sparrow

Purple Finch

Dark-eyed Junco

phased like tilted moons
half shadow, half reflection
juncos cross the snow

five different subspecies around the country—
this one: a slate-colored junco

gray or black hood, white belly, white outer tail feathers

wild turkeys' snow tracks
their arrows point us one way
they go the other

Wild Turkey

males have larger beard, bluish featherless head and neck

distinctive chestnut-
brown tips of tail feathers
(in the Southwest, they're white)

Blue Jay

*black collar, black neck,
black eye line*

calls include hawk imitations, whistles, and gurgles

December's bugler
jay! jay! jay! your one carol
its one gift, the blues

hunkered, plumped sparrow
each feather pockets the heat
a mitten-warmed fist

the bigger the male's bib,
the higher its rank in the group

House Sparrow

dull winter plumage on
both male and female

song: a simple and repetitive
"cheep-cheep-cheep"

raspberry color on male's head/chest
(female is brown, striped)

Purple Finch

song: short warbles: "teh, teh";
sometimes imitates other birds

amazing that these finches even leave tracks—
the heaviest weigh just over one ounce!
their footprints are a metaphor for
the weight of winter, the wait for spring

ice-capped finch feeder
hulls scattered, black snow on white
and the birds' gray weight

Notes for Birdwatchers and Haiku Lovers

Eastern Bluebird

One of the earliest birds to appear in the spring, the eastern bluebird is often thought of as the harbinger of the season. Its song, *truly, truly,* is a soft, garbled series of notes typically sung while flying or feeding. Since groups of bluebirds often rest on power lines that cross meadows, I imagined the lines as a musical staff with these blue quarter notes that run across spring's blue skies.

Canada Goose

A pair of geese preparing to land on a pond call to each other as if maintaining radio contact. Their honking grows louder — *honk, honk, honk* — and more rapid, until, astoundingly, they land — *plop! splat! splash!* (they're big birds, often weighing twenty pounds) — and all the movement goes underwater. Then their webbed feet move them utterly silently through the still water.

American Goldfinch

Goldfinches have the unusual distinction of molting twice during the year, trading in their dull or grayed colors for a dazzling yellow. Some people call goldfinches "wild canaries" because their yellow is as intense as a tropical canary's.

Northern Cardinal

Cardinals pair for life and return to the same nesting ground each year. Even in winter, the male and female both vocalize frequently at their one long meal that begins half an hour before sunrise and ends half an hour after sundown. The birds' round bellies and long tails remind me of quotation marks. I picture the birds like quotes around the sunlight, framing our days as well as theirs.

American Crow

A roost of crows can number two million individuals. Since they're omnivores (eating most everything), they do no small amount of damage to orchards, fields, and crops — yet they also help farmers by eating destructive beetles and grasshoppers. Among the most clever, inquisitive, adaptive, easily trained, and aggressive birds, crows create complex family units, which may include fifteen family members with young from five different years.

Ruby-throated Hummingbird

These hummingbirds migrate from the eastern United States across the Gulf of Mexico and into Central America. They usually return in spring to the same tubular flowers, feeders, and nesting areas, where the females weave tiny nests with strands of spiderwebs. Some birdwatchers say that hummers will buzz at a window to announce their return or to signal that a feeder is out of sugar-water. They're the only birds that can hover in midair or travel backward!

Mourning Dove

Doves are so familiar, it's easy to forget how amazing these creatures are. Unlike most birds, a dove doesn't have to lift its head after each sip to help the water slide down its throat. It's this ability that allows the female to regurgitate a liquid called "pigeon milk" to feed her hatchlings. I meant the poem to suggest that the people watching the nest behind the closed window are also in a kind of shell: they wait for the eggs to hatch and the young to fledge so they can crack open the window again.

Chimney Swift

Found everywhere east of the Rocky Mountains, chimney swifts chit-chatter as they feed on mosquitoes, rarely stopping to perch or rest. They drink, bathe, and even choose twigs for their nests on the wing, and land only at nightfall, often in large groups in or around chimneys. They fly like bats, with stiffly held wings that flap quickly.

Belted Kingfisher

Nearly always found around water, a kingfisher will station itself in a tree along the shore, spot a fish meal below the surface, soar down to the water in a prefect arc, nab the fish in its bill, and swing over to a tree on the opposite bank — like a trapeze artist whose swing touches the net between landing platforms. Perched once again, the kingfisher whacks the fish on the tree and quickly tosses it so that the fish slides, headfirst, down its throat.

Barred Owl

The barred owl's song is described as *who cooks for you, who cooks for you all*. Its call is usually answered by another owl. Some birdwatchers can imitate the owl's call in order to bring an individual owl closer — within range of the binoculars. The owl's sound has been described as a person imitating a monkey imitating a person.

Great Blue Heron

As a heron stalks fish, it steps, stops, steps . . . its webbed feet lifting so carefully that they barely disturb the water. With each step, its thunderbolt-shaped neck compresses or extends. When the heron spots its prey, its bill strikes with lightning speed, stabbing the fish.

Pileated Woodpecker

This poem is the forest's knock-knock joke. The pileated woodpeckers peck at the trees, riddling the trunk as they feed or as they shape their nesting cavities. But curiously, these birds are rarely seen, despite their large size and the loud banging that echoes through the woods. *Knock, knock.* Who's there?

Northern Mockingbird

Mimus polyglottus (mimic of many tongues), the mockingbird, or the American nightingale, isn't the only imitator among the families of birds — but it is the one most likely to keep you awake on a warm July night, especially if there's a full moon and if the bird is a male without a mate. There are records of astounding mockingbirds who can recite three dozen different birdsongs, along with the sounds of other creatures, phones, bells, and various appliances. Most mockingbirds repeat each "verse" or song phrase three or more times.

Common Grackle

Grackles are omnivores — they'll eat acorns, berries, salamanders, grasshoppers, minnows, and even mice. In certain light, a black road can be as iridescent as a grackle. When I saw a grackle in a road's puddle, the scene was like a painting by René Magritte, with elements shifting phases: the asphalt-colored grackle in the grackle-colored asphalt. The haiku holds land and sea and air, one in each of its three lines.

Cedar Waxwing

Nearly always found in a flock, the cedar waxwing is among North America's most frugivorous (fruit-eating) birds. Sugar-rich berries, such as service berries or chokecherries, or the tiny pine seeds of a cedar are its main diet, along with some insects during its late breeding season. Waxwings can devour dozens of fruits and then, later, regurgitate berries into the mouths of nestlings. They also do a version of a bucket brigade, where one bird plucks a fruit, passes it to a nearby bird, who, in turn, passes it to another bird . . . and so on, until some hungry bird just swallows the fruit.

White-breasted Nuthatch

A nuthatch has the singular ability to use its feet to cling to a tree, even upside-down. Searching for seeds or tiny insects, a nuthatch can walk in a spiral along a branch, investigating every niche of bark as if gravity had no influence on its small body. When it finds a sunflower seed or nut, it will jam the morsel into a furrow of tree bark and hammer open the hull with its beak, "hatching" the nutmeat inside. Hence, the name nuthatch.

European Starling

One hundred starlings were brought from Europe and released in New York's Central Park about 115 years ago by Eugene Schieffelin, a member of a society that wanted all birds mentioned in Shakespeare's plays to inhabit the New World. The starling, a member of the mynah family, is a mimic. In *Henry IV, Part I*, Hotspur imagines using a starling to torment Bolingbroke: "Nay, I'll have a starling shall be taught to speak / Nothing but 'Mortimer,' and give it him / To keep his anger still in motion." Even in Shakespeare's day, the starling's uncanny and relentless imitations were well known. Now more than 200 million starlings, many in flocks that exceed 10,000 birds, share this "New World," ranging from Alaska to Florida.

American Robin

The American robin, which can live fourteen years, is the most common thrush in North America. Females can produce three broods in a single year, but only 40 percent of their nests will fill with young, and only a quarter of their fledglings will survive their first autumn. And then it's a long haul through the winter for those individual robins who fail to migrate. They subsist on whatever appears above the snow cover: fruits such as juniper berries, crab apples, or the berries of climbing poison ivy vines.

Black-billed Cuckoo

The cuckoo sings its own name: *cu-cu-cu, cu-cu-cu-cu.* Now rare in the western United States, cuckoos are also known as rain crows because they appear to sing frequently right before a storm. Since cuckoos have a voracious appetite for caterpillars, they tend to stay hidden among branches and brush, where caterpillars are often found. As a result, they're mysterious birds, less often seen than heard.

Dark-eyed Junco

Winter residents, juncos travel in small groups and often visit feeders. Across the country, the coloring of juncos varies slightly, but most have very white under-bellies. In traditional haiku poetry, the poet often looks for a sign of time passing. As juncos hop across the snow, they look like phases of the moon: bird-shaped half moon, quarter moon, crescent moon: a lunar calendar.

Wild Turkey

Wild turkeys often walk the same paths you'd take in the woods. Each print looks like a perfect arrow pressed into the snow, as if the turkeys were showing you the way. But in fact, the arrow's tip is the turkey's heel — the birds are walking in the opposite direction.

Blue Jay

The jay's song is a raucous call, and its blue beauty is just as startling in a different way, especially in a landscape of snow. Some jays migrate; some stay the winter — even the same jay may decide to stay or leave in different years. There's no one simple explanation. The sight of this bird on the snow feels like a small blessing or gift, despite — no, because of — its self-proclaiming caw: *jay, jay, jay.* Or perhaps it's a holiday call of *joy, joy, joy.*

House Sparrow

Fluffing its feathers, a bird creates its own insulation; expanded spaces between the feathers' layers trap in body heat. In colder regions where sparrows overwinter (they're originally from Africa and were introduced in America about 160 years ago), they need this strategy for survival.

Purple Finch

Finches love thistle seeds, which are small, thin, and black. The birds crack the hulls, eat the nut meat inside, and spit out the shells, which fall to the snow — along with plenty of uneaten seeds that ground-feeding birds eat. Opossums, too, come to the feeder at night, extracting whatever nutrition they can from the empty hulls. And then *they* spit out the remains.